Abou

Dr. Dionel Clinton Wa Philadelphia, Pennsylvania. He is the second of five children born to Marion Waters and Darryl Claybourne. Dionel was educated in the Philadelphia Public School System graduating from the Franklin Learning Center. A certified teacher (K-8), principal, and superintendent, Dionel's teaching career spans from Philadelphia, Atlanta, Lansing and Detroit, Michigan, Dallas and Fort Worth, Texas, and internationally in Camden New South Wales, Australia. Dionel served as Principal of Paul L. Dunbar Learning Center, and was an Assistant Principal at Justin F. Kimball High School both in Dallas, Texas. Dionel is currently the principal of a K-8 school, International Leadership of Texas- Arlington Campus which serves over 1,200 students. In addition to serving as a campus principal, Dionel continues to teach at the collegiate level as an Adjunct Professor of Education at Mountainview College and Paul Quinn College. Dionel is a graduate of Morehouse College with a Bachelor of Arts degree in *Elementary Education*, a Master of Arts in *Curriculum and Teaching* from Michigan State University, a dual

Master's of Education degree in *Educational Leadership* and *Business Administration* (MBA) from Dallas Baptist University, and a Ph.D. in *K-16 Educational Leadership and Policy Studies* from the University of Texas at Arlington. Dionel is married to Cynthia Jenae, the Lead Counselor at L.G. Pinkston High School in the Dallas Independent School District. They have two children, Amoi Lei and Dionel Jr. The Waters family resides in Desoto, Texas.

Acknowledgements

First and foremost, all praises go to my Lord and Savior Jesus Christ for His grace and mercy. I am grateful to God that I have been blessed to find my purpose in life. I remember as child being told that "your purpose in life is to find your purpose in life." I have come to realize that my purpose in life is to work with aspiring and beginning principals as they make their transition into the principalship. For that reason, I am truly grateful and I take this "calling" very seriously. Thank you to the following pastors and ministers who instilled in me the love of Christ, Pastor Alpheus Bright, Pastor Richard Bright, Pastor Dr. Myron Barnes, Rev. John Williams, Rev. Samuel Mosteller, Rev. Lee Truss, Rev. Louis Burt, the late Rev. Lester Porter, and Rev. Samuel Wlue.

Throughout my life, I have been blessed with wonderful educators who have impacted my life. This book would not have been possible if it had not been for the teachers I have had during my grade-school matriculation in the School District of Philadelphia. I always talk about the wonderful teachers and principals I had throughout my K-12 experience, but some of my most memorable are Mrs. Barbara Weiss, Mr. Martin Statina, Ms. Joyce Brown, Mr. Ed Grant, Principal Sharif El-Mekki, Principal Charles D'Alfonso, Mr. Roman Kwasnycky, Dr. Alan Lee, Dr. Angela Riley, Mr. Jose Mendez, Mr. Vincent Verderame, Mr. Jeff Chesin, and Principal Charles Staniskis. My K-12 journey includes many other educators who have impacted my life as well. The pages of this book does not warrant enough space for me to name everyone, but please know that your purpose and influence in my life has not gone unnoticed.

My post-secondary education includes the following professors and mentors from Morehouse College, Michigan State University, Dallas Baptist University, and the University of Texas at Arlington who have shaped me into the educator that I am today. These individuals include: Dr. Marcellus Barksdale, Dr. Charles Meadows, Rev. Lee Norris, Dr. Lois Jamison, Dr. Christopher Bass, Morehouse President Dr. Walter Massey, Dr. Christine King-Farris, Dr. Franita Ware, Dr. Marshalita Peterson, Dr. Randi Stanulis, Dr. Sonya Gunnings, Dr. Dorinda Carter-Andrews, Dr. Carol Ames, Dr. Christopher Dunbar, Dr. Carolyn Spain, Principal Chuck Roberts, Dr. Bradley Davis, Dr. Casey Brown, Dr. Sandra Reid, Dr. Ozzie Ingram, Dr. Barbara Tobolowsky, Dr. James Minor, Dr. Curtis

Lewis, Dr. John Lockhart, and Ms. Greta Trice! Thank you all for the scholarly support and career inspiration throughout my educational journey.

As for those who have had a huge impact on my professional career, I want to acknowledge the following people, Superintendent Eddie Conger, Pete Chapasko, Dennis Taylor, Isaac Carrier, Leslie Williams, Earl Jones, Wendy Hawthorne, Maria Freeman, A. Tracie Brown, Takesha Winn, Leticia Gilbert, LaKeisha Smith, Melody Frazier, Corey Harris, and my Australian family Jenny and Liam Murphy (a.k.a. King Tut). When I first became a principal, my job would not have been nearly as productive if it weren't for the following three gentlemen who I owe a great deal of my success to: Quincy Guinyard, Rick Cheatem, and Don Williams. I thank you gentlemen for being my "foot soldiers" in South Dallas!

When it comes to my knowledge of school budgeting and overall campus leadership, I have to thank my former administrative assistant/office manager LaKrystal Greer. We pretty much learned our new roles together and you have no idea how grateful I am to have had you as my "right-hand" during my first principalship. Not only were you a great partner to learn about school leadership with, you were a "big sister" that I always wanted and I am eternally grateful!

Personally, I must acknowledge my family for their constant support and encouragement. I hope this book encourages my siblings, Virgil, Jonell, Marquita, and Desmond, brothers-in-law Christopher and Charles Hawkins, as well as my nieces and nephews to continue working towards their dreams. I am a testament that if you can believe it, you can achieve it! In addition, to the men who have served as "surrogate fathers" in my life, Grandmaster Gregory Slaughter, Deacon Andrew Brunswick, Deacon John Petty, and the late Deacon Isaac Evans. I thank you for showing me what manhood and fatherhood looks like.

A special acknowledgement goes out to a mentor, colleague, and friend Lawrence Galloway. Since moving to Texas, I have admired your teaching style and instructional leadership. You have truly been a role model and "big brother" in the education field to look-up to and I am so appreciative for all that you have contributed to my career. Thank you for also writing the foreword to this book.

To my administrative assistant Ms. Keosha Roy. I can't thank you enough for the support and encouragement that you provide to me on a daily basis. I thank you for listening to all of the thoughts that went through my head during the writing of this book. Thank you for reading and providing feedback on the rough drafts. You have truly been a blessing in my life and I thank you for everything you do for me each and every day.

Finally, none of this would be possible without my rib, my best friend, and my number one support system, my wife Cynthia Jenae. There is not a day that goes by that I am not grateful for having you in my life. You have given me the best gift I could ever imagine in our children (Amoi and Dionel). I thank you for being my "rock" and for all of your sacrifices so that I can do the work that I have been called to do. I love you more than you will ever know!

Dedication

This book is dedicated to the memory of Lillie Lewis, Robert Lewis, Mother Marion S. Waters, and Rev. Dr. Leon A. Waters Jr. I love and miss you all. I hope I have made you all proud! In addition, this book is dedicated to my parents Marion Waters and Darryl Claybourne, God-Mother Veronica T. Clarke, Aunts Christine Lewis, Deborah Caldwell, and Michelle Stevenson, Uncles Arthur (Buster) and the late Clinton Stevenson, God-Parents Jim and Cindy Grant, mother-in-law Beverly Hawkins, father-in-law the late Darrell Andrews, the late Lullaby Andrews, and most importantly my wife Cynthia and children Amoi and Dionel Jr.

Foreword

Its 11:10am and you have just finished a calming response email to a concerned parent. You have five minutes to get to your assigned duty post for the transition of class and for lunch. This is not your favorite time of day and you assigned yourself the tough duty post because you are a "lead-by example" type of principal. You grab your office keys, walkie-talkie, and unfinished orange juice from breakfast. With every step you take, you feel your nerves rise up from your feet because you know the type of commotion you are about to encounter. Your hands are getting sweaty and you wipe them separately on your new pants suit in anticipation for what you know is about to happen, since your first day of standing at this spot 90-days ago.

Your duty post is the intersection of the 6th, 7th, 8th and newly added 9th grade hallway. It is very similar to standing at the intersection of I-635 and I-35 in Dallas, Texas in the middle of July during 5 o'clock traffic. You already know you will have to tell Sean Wilcox to tuck his shirt in. You anticipate having to take Sarah Hinds' cellphone once again, and then debate the cellphone policy with her mother like you do once a month. Sixth graders will be horse playing, engaging in tag, and of course you will have to deal with adolescent hormones. For the life of you, you cannot figure out why the district voted to move 9th grade to a middle school campus and moreover, why your campus? You are a first-year principal and have only lived, breathed, and worked in traditional middle school campuses.

One minute until the bell. You tie your hair back waiting on the rush water of students to hit like it did when you were white water rafting this summer. You can already hear the sounds of the opening and closing of the half lockers that partially work. You close your eyes to meditate for a minute before your adrenaline starts to rush and you have to go into survival mode.

The bell rings. Classroom doors open, but you don't hear anything. Something is different. In every direction you look, you see students in their grade level assigned uniform color walking on the right side of the hallway. You hear inside voice conversation. You only hear a few lockers open and close, and no one asked for assistance. As you stand there stunned and in awe, you try to remember where you are. You haven't had to raise your voice, redirect a student or even take that cellphone you anticipated.

Then, all of a sudden, you see it. A student running at full speed directly towards you. You knew it! It was too good to be true. Somebody was going to pinch you back to reality and you would have to turn back to principal mode and not a stunned mannequin. As you prepare your voice, curl your lips, and wrinkle your forehead, the student yells, "MRS. AKINS! MRS. AKINS! I GOT AN "A" ON MY MATH TEST!!" You respond, "Way to go Erica! I am so proud of you!"

Then it hits you. Your plan worked! All the meetings, conferences, and professional developments you and your team have attended about culture, climate, procedures, routines, and setting high expectations for all students were being displayed. You have tried multiple ways in your building to bring order, but what was different this time was you included your team. From assistant principals, to department chairs, to front office staff, to every single adult in the building. You found a way to ensure everyone was invested and implemented the plan with fidelity. It was a rough first semester, but now you see hope and promise going into the spring semester. More importantly, you see hope and promise for your students and your staff.

Having a plan in place is vitally importantly to the ultimate success of your school building. Just as teachers make bulletin boards, arrange desks, plan lessons and create procedures and routines for their classrooms, principals have to mirror this practice at the campus level. Like teachers, it is better if principals have a plan in place prior to school starting. Will you get it right during your first principalship? What about your second year? You might not, and that is okay. As long as you continue to sharpen your skills, be willing to admit your mistakes, and listen to those who are on the frontline, you will continue to grow and develop your systems and plan for your success as a principal. So, if you are an aspiring principal or new campus leader, this book is for you. The conversational writing style will make you feel as if you are talking to a friend, mentor, or coach as you plan and prepare for your first 90-days. Sit back, enjoy, and utilize this book as if you have a "mentor on standby." It is well worth the investment! Happy Reading!!

Lawrence M. Galloway, J.D.

Lawrence M. Galloway is a graduate of Southern University A&M with a Bachelor of Science degree in Economics and Management. Lawrence holds a Master of Education degree in Education Administration from Texas A&M Commerce and an MBA/Juris Doctorate (JD) from the University of Maryland. A certified principal and superintendent, Lawrence currently works for the Office of the State Superintendent in Washington D.C. as a Management Analyst.

Table of Contents

INTRODUCTION

THIS IS NOT A TEXTBOOK! The intent of this book is not to provide the reader with scholarly literature about school leadership. The sole purpose of this book is to provide novice administrators with practical recommendations that are based on experience as they transition into their new role as campus principals. I was inspired to write this book after my first-year as a principal, because of the constant turnover at the district-level, and the lack of coaching and/or mentoring support I received. As a result, in addition to writing this book, I decided to focus my doctoral dissertation on the perceived impact of coaching and mentoring on the first-year of the principalship. It is easy to see that I am extremely interested and passionate about the type of support first-year principals receive as they transition into their new roles. Ultimately, I wanted to write a book that any new principal (and in some cases experienced administrators) could pick up and turn to specific pages that would provide them with ideas and suggestions to make their first 90-days more manageable. I wanted to focus on the areas of the principalship that would give any new administrator the most leverage as they tackle their first 90-days. These areas include: 1) opening up school/summertime grind, 2) campus culture and climate, 3) instructional leadership, 4) personnel administration (human resources), and 5) school public relations and communications.

I pray that this book will benefit those who are aspiring to become a campus principal and those who are excited about their new journey. Over the course of writing this book, I have received great feedback from many people who have taken these recommendations into job interviews and new campuses with outstanding success. That is the greatest reward and contribution that I could give to the field of education, as well as the personal success I feel when I receive testimonials from implementers. Thank you so much for taking the time to read and utilize this book to your advantage. Good luck as you embark on the rewarding journey known as the principalship.

Dionel C. Waters, Ph.D.

November 2017

Desoto, Texas

CHAPTER 1: OPENING UP SCHOOL (SUMMER GRIND)

You have been given the keys to your campus and now it is time for you to prepare to "Open Up School." What does it mean to "open up school?" How do you "open up school?" Is there a right way or wrong way to "open up school?" How do you ensure that your campus is ready for staff and student arrival? When do you meet with teachers? When do I have time to look at last year's data and create my action plan for this year? When will all of the campus' resources and materials arrive? Reflecting back on the day that I received the keys as principal of Paul Laurence Dunbar Learning Center in Dallas, Texas (which happened to be the same calendar day that Paul L. Dunbar was born) I realized quickly the amount of work I had to do just to get ready for the return of staff and students. There are several different activities that you can engage in to prepare for the opening of school. The purpose of this chapter is to provide you with a few action items that I have found to be the most useful and effective during the "Summertime Grind" as you prepare for your students and staff arrival.

Analyze Last Year's School Data

In order for you to properly prepare for your staff and students' arrival, it is imperative that you analyze your school's data from the previous year (if applicable). This involves looking at student achievement data, teacher performance data, attendance rates (students and staff), number of student referrals, type of student referrals, special education data, bilingual or ESL data (if applicable), graduation and drop-out rates (secondary), student classification based off credits (high school), teacher turnover rate, staff certifications and years of experience data, culture and climate survey results (if applicable), and parent survey results (if applicable). These are the main data points you should consider analyzing prior to your first day with your new staff.

After analyzing your school's previous year data, it is imperative that you create a presentation to present to your staff. Taking the time to analyze the data, create actions steps, and then present it to your staff in a formal meeting is critical. A presentation of this magnitude demonstrates to your staff that you are able to take school data, analyze it, and create action plans based off the data. This is also an opportune time for you to introduce to your staff the key action items, goals, and indicators of success for the upcoming school year.

Welcome & Introduction Letters (Staff, Students, and Families)

As the old adage states, "you only have one time to make a good first impression." One of the best ways to make a good first impression as a new principal is with your welcome letter to your staff and families. In this letter, it is important to describe your educational background, previous professional experiences, a brief description of the vision and mission for the campus, and your excitement to meet everyone in the near future. In addition, I would also recommend that when you send your letter to your staff, you include your summer contact information as well as a couple of days that you will have open to meet with staff members if possible. Nonetheless, you want to take advantage of the opportunity to make a good first impression via a welcome/introduction letter to all of the stakeholders you will work closely with throughout the school year

Individual Meetings with Staff Members

As mentioned in the previous section, if you are able to provide a couple of days to meet with staff members individually over the summer it is very beneficial. I remember when I opened up my schedule (despite how busy I was) to meet individually with staff members to get a "feel" for the campus and to help me with a few action items prior to the start of the school year. My personal belief was, if I spent a few moments learning more about the campus and staff members during the summer, I would save time when school starts from having to learn the same information during the first several weeks of schools. In order for me to maximize my time and effectively create my plan of action, I asked each person the same 4 questions, 1) what worked well, 2) what didn't work, 3) if you could change one thing immediately what would it be, and 4) what are your expectations of me as principal? I purposely asked those same questions to each person in order for me to determine some common trends. I wanted to know what are the things that the staff considered effective, those things that were ineffective, and if there were any commonality among the "number one thing" they would change immediately. Finally, going into a campus as a new principal, it was also important for me to know what the expectations of me were and how I could mentally prepare myself as I embarked on this journey as a new campus leader.

Meet with Campus Leadership Team

As a new campus principal, it is imperative that you spend some time during the summer meeting with your leadership team. Keep in mind that your leadership team is not limited to your assistant principal(s). Meaning, there may be teacher-leaders on campus, school counselors, influential teacher assistants or paraprofessionals, instructional coaches, anyone on campus that has a huge impact on your ability to influence staff morale, raise student achievement, and ultimately accomplish the goals of the campus.

Prior to meeting with your campus leadership team, ensure that you spend the necessary time preparing for this very important meeting. Remember, you are only given one opportunity to make a good first impression, and that fact is no different when it comes to meeting with your campus leadership team. Spend time gathering data from the previous year and conduct your own individual analysis. Prepare guiding questions that you will share with your leadership team and have them analyze campus data. Be sure to compare their findings to what you have as you begin to calibrate and align your frameworks for teaching and learning.

As the "new kid on the block," your analysis will focus mostly on the quantifiable results. The beauty of having your leadership team analyze the data with you, is their ability to provide you with the qualitative/narrative data that is not evident in the "numbers" such as the instructional capacity and years of experience of the teachers, professional mindset, classroom set-up, etc. Having access to the qualitative/narrative data from your leadership team, helps create the context for the quantitative numbers. Do not overestimate the importance of having both quantitative and qualitative data at the forefront of your analysis especially when creating academic goals for the upcoming year.

In addition to analyzing data and creating campus goals, it is equally important for you to learn more about the strengths and weaknesses of your campus leadership team. These are the individuals that you must "lean on" during the school year in order to accomplish the goals of the campus. Being able to strategically and purposefully utilize each of your teammates' strengths in a cohesive manner is critical to the success of the campus and your success as a principal. One of the first things you will learn as a principal is that you cannot effectively do this job alone. You are going to need the support and dedication from every team member, so familiarizing yourself with your leadership team's strengths and knowing when it is best to utilize them, is one of the most important roles of being a principal.

The goal of the summer campus leadership team meeting is for you to analyze campus data, learn more about the strengths and weaknesses of your leadership team members, and to ultimately conclude the meeting with an action plan. Your action plan (based off the data), should reflect S.M.A.R.T. (specific, measurable, attainable, realistic, and timely) goals, specific action steps in order to achieve those goals, and indicators of success that easily determines if your goals have been accomplished. Of course the first meeting is not intended to have a finalized end-all version of the action plan. This time together should be considered a meeting of the minds that will allow for the leadership team to build a solid foundation, have a strong direction when the school year starts, and most importantly a "working" document that the team can revisit as needed throughout the year.

Finalize Handbooks for Staff and Students

One of your biggest guides as a new principal will be your campus handbook. It is imperative that you take the necessary time preparing and finalizing the handbooks for both staff and students prior to their arrival. The use of a student handbook is usually dependent on the grade levels of your campus, but nearly all campuses will utilize a staff handbook. This staff handbook should highlight your expectations for the year as well as reiterate the common procedures and processes for the campus. Your staff handbook does not have to be large in size, as long as it focuses the reader on the most important aspects of the campus. Having a staff handbook allows for you to reference specific parts during the school year when necessary. I also recommend keeping a saved electronic copy of the handbook readily available so you can make any necessary changes/updates during the year or in preparation for the upcoming school year.

Meet with your School Board Representative

Despite what many people outside of education (and some inside) may think, summertime is very busy for principals as they prepare for the upcoming school year. For new principals, that busy feeling is amplified as you prepare for the upcoming year with little information or contextual foundation. One thing that I would highly recommend for new principals if at all possible, is to carve out some time to meet with your school board representative. School board members are very busy people who can have a major impact on your success as a principal. The involvement of School Board members with principals varies by school districts, so it is imperative that you learn the "School Board Culture" as soon as possible. Spend the necessary time getting to know your school board representatives and share with them the vision and goals that you have for the campus. Remember them during "School Board Appreciation Month" and do something special for them. When your campus achieves certain milestones (small or large) share the news with your school board representative. They will be able to speak to constituents about the great things happening on your campus. In addition to the superintendent, it is always good to have a positive professional relationship with your school board representative.

Meet with Local Businesses, Religious Institutions, and Community Leaders

In addition to scheduling time to meet with your school board representative, it is equally important to meet with local businesses, religious institutions, and community leaders in order to establish positive relationships and productive partnerships. As a new principal, you may not know all of the "important" community leaders, but rest assure, they will find out about the new principal and want to meet with you. As previously mentioned, the summertime is very busy for new principals so in the midst of all of your meetings, trainings, and prepping for the upcoming school year, schedule time to meet with local leaders and explain your vision and goals for your campus. These meetings can follow the same format as the meeting with the school board representative, but during this meeting you may want to have a response ready when the local leaders ask how they can possibly help partner with the school during the year. Take advantage of those opportunities to build lasting relationships with community leaders that are willing and able to provide assistance throughout the school year. Designate someone on your campus to serve as the volunteer coordinator in order to track all partnerships and provide you with updates throughout the year. Partnerships such as these, are not only beneficial to your students, but they also serve as a marketing component for your campus within the community.

Finalize Master Schedule and Student Rosters

Any effective administrator will tell you that the "heartbeat" of a great school is the master schedule. It is imperative that the master schedule is coherent, logical, systematic, and addresses the needs of the students. Prior to the first week of school, you want to ensure that your master schedule is complete and free of errors. As a former high school assistant principal, I am very familiar with the importance of having a well-structured and coordinated master schedule. That is why when I became an elementary school principal, I was adamant about creating the schedule personally and not leaving it to chance with anyone else. When you are able to create and visualize the implementation of your master schedule, you are on the right track.

After your "error-free" master schedule is complete with the sequence of courses, it is time to start thinking about the teaching capacity of your staff and specific certifications. Based on teaching certifications and capabilities, you are going to identify staff members for certain teaching positions. Once the teaching positions are secured, and you have verified your master schedule for 100% accuracy, then you are ready to confirm student rosters. First and foremost, your master schedule has to be in place before student rosters can be verified and confirmed. When confirming student rosters, you want to keep in mind the type of course (traditional, advanced placement, remedial, dual-credit, etc.) being offered. Afterwards, you must consider the student-teacher ratio for each course. You want to be mindful of not having too many students in one class without the proper teacher coverage. This is especially important for high school master schedules. At the high school level, you want to ensure that you have enough sections of a particular course so that the student-teacher ratio is not too high, and students have the opportunity to receive credit for courses needed. The overall goal in creating your master schedule, and verifying/confirming student rosters, is to ensure that every student has a schedule that fits their academic needs on the first day of school.

Regular Check-Ins with Custodial Staff

In the midst of preparing to open up school, it is important to conduct regular check-ins with your custodial staff. Prior to your teachers returning to campus, you want to have all classrooms cleaned and the building ready to receive students and visitors. In order to ensure that this takes place, it is imperative that you walk your building on a daily basis to monitor summer cleaning progress and make any last minute recommendations to the custodial staff. Having a clean building prior to staff returning and in preparation of the first day of school is critical to your ability to make a great first impression.

Meet the Principal Night

The last piece of advice that I will give regarding effective ways to utilize your summer prior to the start of your new principalship is to host a "Meet the Principal Night." This is a great opportunity to meet with community leaders, campus staff, students, family members, etc. During this event, have refreshments available and walk around informally to meet and greet your stakeholders. This is a perfect time for your stakeholders to meet you "the person" and not necessarily "the principal." Throughout the year they will get to know you "the principal" so utilize this time to have people get to know who you are as an individual. Also, keep in mind the importance of having some time set-aside for you to speak about your campus vision, goals, and expectations for the year. You will have many stakeholders at this event wanting to learn more about your goals for the campus, so take advantage of the opportunity to get your message across early in your tenure. Don't feel pressured to speak in depth about your vision (you will have more than enough opportunities to do so throughout the year) just keep your message short, sweet, and straight to the point.

Monthly Incentives and Celebrations

As a new elementary school principal, I learned quickly the importance of having monthly incentives and celebrations. These monthly events would include incentives such as, jeans/dress down days, spirt days, Black History month, Cinco De Mayo, Asian-American Heritage Month, etc. Not only were these events cherished at the elementary level, as a high school assistant principal, my staff and students enjoyed them as well. Therefore, it is very important that as a new principal you work with your secretary to map out a calendar of events so that everyone is included.

After mapping out the events, I would recommend that you designate certain people on your staff to take lead with creating and organizing the celebrations. Your job as principal is extremely demanding and time-consuming. You will need other staff members to step up and assist you with the events. Let them take lead and build their leadership capacity. This will help you in the future. As principal, I recommend that you acknowledge special events and provide a space and an opportunity for staff members to be creative in their approach to celebrating them. Ensure that your staff understands that you have given them "defined autonomy" to take lead with the event. This includes checking in with them periodically to verify progress towards completion. Finally, let them know that you are willing and able to help in whatever capacity needed. This will reassure to your staff that you trust them, you are going to hold them accountable for doing a great job, but ultimately you are going to be supportive. Having that approach works well when establishing a positive culture and climate on your campus, while also building leadership capacity.

As a new principal there are three events that you definitely do not want to forget: administrative assistant day, teacher appreciation week, and school board recognition month. Administrative assistant day is usually in the spring, so don't forget this important day for obvious reasons! ☺ In the state of Texas teacher appreciation week is usually the first week in May and school board recognition month is in January. Place these events on your calendar early and begin thinking of staff members that can assist you with these events. It is worth the time and energy. TRUST ME!!

Extra-Curricular Activities (Academic & Athletic)

Extra-curricular activities are important for any campus. Through academic and athletic activities, students are able to become more confident in their abilities as well as build solid relationships that may last a lifetime. As a new principal, it is imperative that you allow for students to engage in extra-curricular activities. Whenever possible, make time to attend an academic and/or athletic event. Your presence at these events, will send a positive message to your staff and community, but most importantly your students. Words cannot express how excited my students would get and how great I felt when I attended one of their events. During these events, I am fully attentive to what is happening and I am my campus' biggest cheerleader! In addition to providing social and academic opportunities for your students, extra-curricular activities are a great way to build positive morale and campus pride which ultimately influences your school's culture and climate. So get out there, new principal, and become your campus' number one fan! It will be worth it in the end!

Closing Thought

As you can see opening up school is a very busy time. Nonetheless, it is very important to do it the "RIGHT WAY." Make sure you spend time getting into your school's data from the previous year (if applicable). This will allow for you to start thinking about your game plan for the new academic year. Introduce yourself to your staff and stakeholders with a welcome letter. Ensure that you open up your schedule to make time to meet with people (staff, school board representative, community members, etc.) who would like to introduce themselves to you. Schedule your "Meet the Principal" night as soon as possible. This event will allow for parents and students to meet you informally prior to the first day of school. Despite all of the hustle and bustle during your summertime grind, you will need to spend time with your campus leadership team. Schedule time to conduct walk-throughs with your custodial team to ensure that your building is ready to receive students and staff. Most importantly, make sure that your campus' master schedule is error-free and every student has a schedule prior to the first-day of school.

CHAPTER 2: CULTURE & CLIMATE

As a new principal, I had to learn quickly the role that culture and climate play in the type of campus I wanted to create. Dr. Kent D. Peterson, a professor in the Department of Educational Administration at the University of Wisconsin-Madison defines school culture as "the set of norms, values and beliefs, rituals and ceremonies, symbols and stories that make up the 'persona' of the school." School climate is defined as "the quality and character of school life. School climate is based on patterns of students, parents and school personnel's experience of school life and reflects norms, goals, values, interpersonal relationships, teaching and learning practices, and organizational structures" (National School Climate Center).

Personally, I define campus culture as "the way we DO things around here." I define campus climate as "how one FEELS when they are around here." Understanding the importance of culture and climate was critical as I began my journey as a new campus principal. The purpose of this chapter is to provide recommendations on how to establish and maintain the type of culture and climate you desire for your campus during the first 90-days.

School Vision and Mission Statements

The foundation of your campus should be rooted in your school's vision and mission. Every campus should have a vision and mission statement. School Vision is defined as "a public declaration used to describe a school's high level goals for the future and what they hope to achieve if they successfully fulfill their organizational purpose or mission" (Glossary of Education Reform). School Mission is defined as "a written declaration of an organization's core purpose and focus that normally remains unchanged over time" (businessdictionary.com). One of the first things you should convey to your staff is the importance of your campus' vision and mission. Once you are named principal, it is critical for you to begin thinking about the type of campus you want to create. If possible, spend some time over the summer working with your campus leaders to create the mission and vision statements if needed. Working collaboratively with your leadership team on the creation of the campus' vision and mission statements will help with staff buy-in. As a principal, you cannot take for granted the importance of staff buy-in because ultimately these are the individuals who are going to help you spread the message behind the mission and vision.

After finalizing the campus' mission and vision statements, it is your responsibility as principal to work diligently to get your staff to internalize those beliefs and use them as a guide when making daily decisions. Take advantage of every opportunity to reiterate your campus' vision and mission. There are certain things that you can do as principal to reiterate your vision and mission. In the past, I have placed the campus' vision and mission statements on professional development and staff meeting agendas, newsletters, weekly memos, morning announcements, etc. My goal was to have every staff member and student on the campus internalize and be able to articulate the campus' vision and mission statements when asked. I never wanted a district-level employee (superintendent, assistant superintendent, coordinator, etc.) to come on campus and ask my staff about our vision and mission and they were unable to reiterate our beliefs through their words and/or actions.

As a new principal, it will take time to get your staff to memorize the vision and mission statements. In addition to having staff memorize the campus' vision and mission statements, it is equally important for them to internalize the message. Remember to always remain consistent and persistent in your quest to create a campus that is grounded in a vision and mission that has the best interest of students at its core.

School Year Theme

As previously mentioned, having both a vision and mission statement for your campus is critical as you set the foundation for the school year. In addition to your vision and mission statements, having a "School Year Theme," is a great way to rally your campus around a centralized focus for the year. School year themes are usually short phrases such as "one team, one dream," "fired up," "shooting for the stars," etc. In addition to having a school year theme memorized and reiterated each day through morning/closing announcements, you can decorate your campus around the theme so staff, students, and visitors can become familiar with the campus focus for the year. This is a great way to triangulate your campus' yearly theme, culture and climate, while getting your staff members on board with the direction in which the campus is headed.

Grade Level Assemblies

The first day of school is here and as a new principal the only question you have on your mind is, how do I convey my expectations to all students in one day? On the first day of school, after the classes have been in session for about an hour and the building is beginning to reflect a calm environment, I would start my grade level assemblies. During this period, I introduce the campus' academic and behavioral expectations for the year. Time spent on the grade level assemblies during the first day of school is important and valuable because all of the students in a specific grade level(s) will hear from the principal. In addition to having your students present at the assembly, please ensure that your staff attends. Staff members need to hear the same information as the students. By having students and staff in the grade level assembly, you are able to hold both groups accountable because they are hearing the same information at the same time. The best part of this session, is your ability to clear up any misunderstandings and answer any questions that staff and students may have regarding the campus' academic and behavioral expectations.

Culture and Climate Committee

It is evident that a campus' culture and climate are important factors for new principals to consider when creating the type of atmosphere that is conducive to teaching and learning. If a principal does not establish a strong culture and climate at the very beginning, they can ultimately still reach their goals, but at what expense? In order to combat the risk of not establishing a strong culture and climate early in the school year, new principals should consider creating a culture and climate committee. Granted, as a new principal you may not be aware of the best candidates for the committee, nonetheless, through your summer interviews/meetings with staff members, you can determine who may be a good fit. Acknowledge their influence as an informal or formal leader on campus and request their participation as a committee member. This is another opportune time to seek input from your leadership team to see who may be a great candidate for the committee.

When establishing your campus culture and climate, it is critical for you to influence the informal and formal leaders. After assembling your committee, take the necessary time throughout the year (biweekly or monthly) to meet with your team in order to get a continuous pulse of your building and to think of opportunities to "celebrate" and show appreciation for your staff. What may seem as a small or little gesture can go a long way in maintaining a positive culture and climate on your campus.

Staff Recognitions

I am sure that we all can agree that when we are recognized for a job well done it is a great feeling. This is no different for your staff who work tirelessly on a daily basis. As a new principal, taking the time to recognize your high performers during staff meetings and on a monthly basis, will yield huge benefits for you and your campus' culture and climate. As principal, I did a few things to recognize my staff on a consistent basis. First, during our weekly staff meetings, I would recognize individuals with the ABCD (Above and Beyond the Call of Duty) Award. This award was given to staff members who went above and beyond their regular job duties to ensure that the campus functioned effectively and efficiently. I also allowed for other staff members to recognize their colleagues which made giving and receiving this award really special!

Each month I would recognize the teacher and staff member of the month. As principal, I wanted to do something a little different than the typical teacher of the month (which would eliminate your support staff each time), so I decided to do both teacher and support person recognitions. I would have teachers and support staff vote for their colleagues and the staff members with the most votes (one teacher and one support staff) would be the winners for the month. During teacher appreciation week, I would have lunch catered for the staff and they would vote for the teacher and support person of the year. This was an opportunity for the staff to select, not the administrative team, the teacher and support person of the year. I am proud to say that each year my teacher of the year received a gift card (Southwest Airlines) to fly anywhere they desired, and my support person of the year received a weekend stay at the Omni Hotel. I am not recommending that you spend a lot of money on the campus' teacher and support person of the year awards, but I highly encourage any principal to take the time to recognize their staff as much as possible.

Campus Newsletter

Establishing and maintaining open communication with your stakeholders is very important. As principal, I knew that my stakeholders wanted to hear from me on a regular basis. Therefore, the best way to keep that communication consistent was through a weekly newsletter. I personally felt that it was important for my stakeholders to know that each week on a specific day (which happened to be Tuesday on my campus), they could expect some type of communication from me. My school's mascot at Dunbar was a Jaguar. Therefore, every Tuesday I would send home a copy of the Jaguar Journal (campus newsletter) that I personally wrote each week in English and Spanish.

Each newsletter contained a personal message from me, a campus update, a special "shout-out for students and staff, a college highlight, and a calendar of events. Not only did the weekly newsletter keep my stakeholders informed, it also decreased the amount of time I had to spend reiterating and reminding people of what was happening on the campus. Despite the amount of time it takes to create, I highly recommend new principals to establish some form of communication (hard copy or electronic) that they will use on a weekly basis to keep all stakeholders informed of the great things that are happening on the campus.

Closing Thought

Having a strong vision and mission for your campus is imperative as you embark on your journey. In addition to your vision and mission, think of a creative "theme" for the school year that can get you and your staff excited. When identified, have your staff decorate the campus around that centralized theme for reinforcement throughout the year. The school year is very long and there will be times when students and staff feel exhausted. Consider creating a "Culture and Climate Committee" that will be responsible for different events throughout the year for students and staff in order to keep the morale high. Any effective principal will tell you that consistent and transparent communication with stakeholders is critical. Think of ways to keep the lines of communication open so that information is reaching the masses in a timely manner. When establishing a strong culture and climate, don't overlook the importance of having grade level assemblies during the first day or week of school to reiterate academic and behavioral expectations.

CHAPTER 3: INSTRUCTIONAL LEADERSHIP

The principalship has changed drastically from a position that
has traditionally focused on compliance and operations, to a stronger
focus on teaching and learning. With a stronger emphasis on
academic accountability at a national level, it only makes sense that
school leaders are prepared to address the many facets of
instructional leadership. Despite this "paradigm shift" as it relates to
the major role of the principal, campus leaders are still held
accountable for the daily managerial aspects of the principalship. In
order to do this well, it is imperative that principals understand the
importance of time management, while continuing to have most of
their attention dedicated to instructional leadership. This chapter
will focus on the different components of instructional leadership
and the responsibility of the principal to align their instructional
leadership team for the benefit of increasing student academic
achievement.

Administrators & Instructional Coach(es) Alignment

One of the greatest assets for any principal instructionally is their
instructional coach.

I learned this firsthand as an assistant principal at Justin F. Kimball High School. During my tenure at Kimball, I felt as if we had the best instructional coaches ever. We had a team of coaches (one for each of the four major content areas) that would go above and beyond to ensure that teachers had what they needed in order for students to be successful academically. Even though our school district was moving towards principals and assistant principals becoming more "instructionally-sound," the coaches that we had really made that transition easier for everyone. At that moment in my life, I felt as if I was blessed to be around so many talented educators.

Despite having instructional coaches that were well-versed in their disciplines and capable of working effectively with teachers, as a principal, I had to learn the importance of having alignment with your instructional coaches. During the summer months, it will be imperative for you to meet with your instructional leadership team. This team should include your assistant principals and instructional coaches. As principal, it will be critical for you to discuss with your Instructional Leadership Team (ILT) your vision for the campus instructionally, the campus' goals, and the role that each person will play in order to reach those goals. You will need to decide if you are going to assign your assistant principals and instructional coaches to specific grade levels or content areas. This decision is very important as it relates to alignment, but must be made as a "campus-based decision" because all campuses are different and so are their instructional needs. In addition, I highly recommend meeting with your ILT on a weekly basis in order to discuss instructional trends, recommend any professional developments, analyze data, etc. By meeting each week, you are working cohesively as an instructional leadership team to align responsibilities in order to meet and/or exceed academic achievement goals.

Curriculum Alignment (Written, Taught, and Tested)

If student achievement is going to improve in any school, strong alignment must exist between the written curriculum (state standards), instructional strategies used in the classroom (purposeful instruction), and how those standards are assessed/tested at the campus, district, and state levels. I am a firm believer in curriculum alignment. It requires the teacher to spend more time planning and becoming a "content expert" upfront, but the payoff is astronomical in the end when done correctly. Curriculum alignment embodies the idea of "planning with the end in mind." Meaning, curriculum alignment requires the teacher to understand how students are going to be assessed according to the content standards. Then the teacher prepares their instruction in a manner that will ensure that their students not only learn the content standards, but are able to answer assessment questions that are aligned to those standards. Teachers and students can't help but to be successful when curriculum alignment is evident throughout the campus. Curriculum alignment is a great way to reinforce purposeful and intentional instruction, because the teacher knows exactly what their end goal is and the action steps needed in order to meet or exceed those goals.

Professional Learning Communities (PLCs)

When it comes to instructional leadership, the second most important initiative that a principal should monitor aside from curriculum alignment are professional learning communities (PLCs). As a principal, I along with my instructional coaches and assistant principals, would engage in professional learning communities each week with teachers. These weekly meetings which took about 40 minutes, focused on instructional planning and preparation, common assessments, data analysis, action planning, and examining student work. I am a firm believer that alongside curriculum alignment, professional learning communities are very impactful when it comes to student achievement. Time is spent each week with teachers getting together to collaborate and brainstorm "best practices" as it relates to student learning. Instructional coaches play a huge role in PLCs because they are able to probe teachers' thinking while also providing content expert advice and recommendations. The administrator's role is just as important because they are tasked with putting systems in place that will allow for teachers to implement best practices without outside barriers getting into the way. Time spent in professional learning communities planning both vertically and horizontally across the content, coupled with strong curriculum alignment is a great combination to have when increasing student achievement.

When structuring professional learning communities (PLCs), I have always found it helpful to focus on the following four questions introduced by Dufour (2011): 1) what do we expect our students to learn (content standards), 2) how will we know they are learning (assessment), 3) how will we respond when they don't learn (intervention), and 4) how will we respond when they learn it (enrichment)?

Progress Monitoring (Data-Driven Decision Making)

A chapter on instructional leadership would not be complete without discussing the importance of progress monitoring. I wanted to include this section immediately after professional learning communities because progress monitoring focuses on data gathering, data analysis, and making informed decisions based off the data. As the instructional leader of a campus, it is imperative that you are aware of where your students are academically according to their data. This is especially true when preparing them for state assessments. Meaning, you should consider creating interim assessments (3week-6week periods) where you are able to assess your students with an aligned instrument (aligned to the state's standards and assessment) in order to determine their academic shortcomings. This data and information should be gathered and analyzed within 48 hours of assessment completion. The data will not serve any substantial purpose if it is not analyzed in a timely manner.

In addition to analyzing the data and determining where the shortcomings are, it is equally important for you to create an action plan that addresses the low standards with the intent of re-teaching and reassessing. You don't want to wait until the last minute to determine that many of your students did not master specific standards and then try to "cram" all of the information in at the last minute. One of my former Assistant Superintendents always referred to it as "stopping the bleeding early." Despite the gruesomeness of the analogy, it really summarizes the main intention of getting the data that you need quickly and doing something about immediately. You can't leave those standards to "chance" as you prepare your students for state assessments.

Classroom Observations and Instructional Feedback

As previously mentioned, in this new age of academic accountability, the role of the principal has transitioned from one that focused mainly on operations to becoming more of an instructional leader. As a result, it is imperative that principals find time to get into classrooms and conduct observations. Principals can't truly know what is going on in their schools as it relates to teaching and learning unless they spend time in classrooms. I ultimately keep this golden question in mind when conducting classroom observations: "how can we improve instruction for that specific period in time?" This question helps to focus my attention on specific areas related to teaching and learning during my observation.

Observing instruction is critical when trying to raise academic achievement, but equally important, is the instructional feedback that teachers receive from administrators and/or instructional coaches once the observations are complete. As a principal, there are three things that I always keep in mind as it relates to classroom observations. Those three things are: 1) classroom observations are conducted on a regular basis, 2) instructional feedback is "bite-size" and measureable, and 3) the follow-up observation is just as important as the initial observation or instructional feedback provided.

First, classroom observations should be conducted on a regular basis. When principals are able to get into classrooms and observe instruction regularly, they are able to determine instructional trends and therefore provide professional development accordingly. This is a great way for principals to begin tailoring the type of support they provide to teachers based off what they are seeing in classrooms.

Second, instructional feedback should be "bite-size" and measureable. A common mistake that many principals make when providing instructional feedback to teachers is the tendency to provide too many action steps in which the teacher becomes overwhelmed and no changes are made. After each observation and instructional feedback session, I would focus on the "bite-size" feedback. Meaning, what are those action items that teachers could quickly change and implement in their classroom immediately or within a short period of time, that can serve as a leverage point in raising student achievement. As a principal, I am adamant about providing my teachers with instructional next steps that would benefit teaching and learning. Instructional next steps that can be implemented quickly, as opposed to providing them with a long "laundry-list" of pedagogical action items.

Finally, the follow-up observation is just as important as the initial observation or instructional feedback provided. The first two steps (observation and feedback) are pretty easy to implement for administrators. For the most part, administrators understand the importance of conducting classroom observations and providing instructional feedback. Many administrators would admit that they are able to observe instruction and provide timely feedback on a consistent basis. The challenge is the follow-up observation. In other words, when providing teachers with timely, bite-size feedback, you should inquire with the teacher on when those action items are going to be implemented into their classroom. After getting the date and possibly the time, administrators must work extremely hard (among the many other tasks they are responsible for each day) to get back into the classroom to assess and debrief about the effectiveness of the implementation.

In-House Professional Development (Instructional Trends)

As the instructional leader of the campus, it is your responsibility to get into classrooms, observe instruction, and identify instructional trends despite the support you may receive from assistant principals and/or instructional coaches. The main benefit of getting into classrooms and identifying instructional trends, would be your increased ability to conduct in-house professional development depending on campus need. Sending teachers to trainings and professional development sessions are great investments, if teachers are able to take what they have learned and apply it to the classroom setting. Many times, professional development sessions are "hit or miss." When you are able to specifically identify the professional development needed on your campus and bring in people who can assist, or have people on the campus create the professional development sessions, you are taking advantage of a key leverage point. In order to take advantage of this key leverage point, you must understand and be able to identify the instructional trends on your campus and get your teachers the support they need quickly.

In addition, as the instructional leader on the campus, after the support has been given to the teachers through professional development, it is your responsibility to ensure that whatever has been discussed and modeled through the professional development, is evident in the classroom. This approach increases the level of accountability for the teacher and administrator when determining if the professional development was worth the investment.

Closing Thought

The role of the principal has changed. During this era of increased accountability for student performance, the principalship has a much stronger focus on instructional leadership. Three areas that any new or experienced principal should focus on are 1) curriculum alignment, 2) PLCs, and 3) progress monitoring. Those three areas when aligned and done well, can result in students achieving at high academic levels. In addition to those three components of instructional leadership, ensuring that you conduct classroom observations, provide timely instructional feedback, and coordinate professional development trainings based off instructional trends/needs will also help increase student academic performance.

CHAPTER 4: SCHOOL PERSONNEL ADMINISTRATION
(HUMAN RESOURCES)

If I was given the opportunity to give every new principal one piece of advice, it would be to "ensure that you hire well!" Even though, hiring well has its many benefits that can make your job as a principal very enjoyable and less stressful, hitting the "lottery" with personnel is not always the case. Unless you are really sure about a potential candidate, you are always taking a chance when recommending someone for hire. Therefore, knowing that recommending someone for hire is one of the most important decisions you will make as a principal, please refrain from rushing the process.

I remember one of my former superintendents putting a demand/directive on all campus principals to have ZERO vacancies on the first day of school. Despite how important that is, and understanding the logic behind that approach, if that means rushing a hiring decision for the sake of having no vacancies when the doors of the school open up, I don't agree with that methodology. When hiring someone you really want to take the time to determine if that person aligns with the vision that you have for the campus, is willing to have a collaborative spirit when working with the school staff, and if they will be a "good fit" for the school and community. As previously stated, you want to "ensure that you hire well" if given the opportunity to hire staff members. If you are not in a position as a new principal to hire any staff members, spend the time observing and getting to know your staff in order to determine who needs additional support or if you need to replace anyone. If the decision is to replace someone, begin compiling the necessary documentation in order to move quickly and professionally when recommending someone for termination or non-renewal. More on the topic of documentation and termination/non-renewal recommendations later in the chapter.

First-Year= Learn EVERY Staff Member For Yourself

The second best piece of advice when I got my first principal job didn't come from a former principal nor a superintendent; it actually came from my mother-in-law. She had just retired from working in the Dallas Independent School District for over 30 years and the advice she gave me was to spend the first-year "learning every staff member for yourself." Before you go in and make any huge changes, learn the systems and structures that are already in place as well as the people working there. Of course, if there are situations where the safety and well-being of children is compromised (I had that my first-year), then you must address those predicaments quickly according to district policy. In other cases, take the time to learn who are your 1) high-will/high ability, 2) low-will/high ability, 3) high-will/low ability, and 4) low-will/low ability staff members. Spending time identifying specific individuals that fit into one of the four tiers and then responding accordingly prior to the end of the first-year, will make your second year a lot easier.

It comes without question that you are going to have both high and low performers on your staff. You are going to have those who are there for the right reasons and those who are basically "collecting a check." Those individuals who are there "collecting a check" and are unable or unwilling to change, require a different type of conversation. These individuals are the ones that you want to get off your campus prior to the beginning of the next school year. As I mentioned before, "act quickly and professionally."

A very special note: there is a huge possibility that your first principalship will be at a school that already has a staff in place. Therefore, you will be inheriting a staff that you did not have anything to do with in regards to hiring. Even though I am advocating the idea of spending the necessary time to get to know your staff for yourself, it will not take long for you to determine those staff members who are "not going to make it." What I would highly recommend in this case so that you are able to start afresh with a new person the following year, is to contact your human resources department as soon as possible and learn about the process needed to recommend termination for an employee. YES, you want to get to know your staff for yourself. YES, you want to work and assist those in need, but ultimately you are responsible for the teaching and learning that goes on in your building and that requires making difficult decisions at times, which can lead to the termination of an employee's contract. Nonetheless, if you find yourself in a situation where you are working with the human resources department to recommend termination of an employee's contract, remember to remain professional throughout the entire process, adhere to all deadlines and guidelines, and be as transparent as possible with the staff member.

Utilize Strengths and Support Opportunities to Strengthen Weaknesses

After spending the time to get to know your staff members personally, you are going to be able to identify those high-performers who go above and beyond the call of duty to ensure student academic success. Whenever possible, take the time to acknowledge those individuals (both privately and publicly) by letting them know how much you care about them and appreciate their commitment to improving academic achievement. Utilize their strengths to assist other teachers or to help with activities around the campus.

When utilizing your high-performers because of their tremendous skillset, be very careful of not "over-utilizing" them. Meaning, many high-performers feel overwhelmed when they are constantly being asked to commit to additional responsibilities without getting anything "taken off their plate." If at all possible, whenever requesting additional responsibilities from your high-performers, consider other areas where you can take the "load off" in order to compensate them for being a team player and going above and beyond their job descriptions. The last thing you want to do as a principal is to have your high-performers feeling overworked because they are taking up the slack for some of your low-performing staff members.

In addition to those high-performers, you are going to have staff members who will need opportunities to strengthen their capacity in certain areas. Those staff members who are struggling, but have the desire and dedication to do well, should be given the necessary support and development to improve their craft. While providing them with that support, make it a priority to check in periodically to ensure that the support is working and if there are areas that need readjusting. Those individuals who are low-skill/high-will are usually appreciative of the support and will work hard to improve their craft for the sake of their students' academic success. I am a huge proponent for supporting teachers who are trying to grow professionally. On the other hand, you will have some staff members who could care less about growing professionally for the benefit of their students, and those individuals require a different type of conversation.

Crucial Conversations and Documentation

When you finally take that seat in the principal's chair, you can rest assure that a crucial conversation is not far behind. I define a crucial conversation as a "high stakes discussion with strong emotions." Throughout my tenure as principal, I have found myself engaging in more crucial conversations with staff members than any other group. On any given day, I can rest assure that I will need to have at least one crucial conversation with a staff member. These staff members include those on the campus leadership team, to custodians working diligently to keep the campus immaculate. Despite the role and responsibilities of the staff member, crucial conversations require a certain amount of time and attention in order to be productive.

There are four guiding principles that I adhere to and would recommend to any school leader when it comes to having crucial conversations with staff members. These four guidelines are 1) be willing to have crucial conversations, 2) know your communication style, 3) be transparent, honest, and ethical, and 4) keep your eyes on the prize: what's best for students (Waters, 2017). As a principal, I had to understand that even though I may not enjoy having crucial conversations, they were needed in order to ensure that my staff understood the importance of our work; which was to improve student academic achievement. Without question, you are going to have times when crucial conversations are needed because of "adult drama," but nonetheless, the ultimate goal even in the midst of the drama is to refocus our attention on doing what's best for children.

In addition to having crucial conversations, providing the staff member with follow-up documentation is equally important and a great practice to start early-on in your career. One of my most famous mantras as a principal is "DOCUMENTATION BEATS CONVERSATION ANY DAY OF THE WEEK!!" Document anything and everything! Despite how tedious and burdensome it may feel; it will be well worth the journey in the end. I cannot begin to explain how much documentation has helped me with many different situations throughout my career. Since I was able to have good documentation when it came to different events, I didn't have to worry about remembering anything or getting facts twisted. In other words, the "documentation spoke for itself."

Here are a few tips that I keep in mind when documenting: 1) use letterhead when documenting formally, 2) state the facts in your documentation, 3) reference district policy (legal/local), 4) DO NOT WRITE DOWN YOUR FEELINGS JUST STRAIGHT FACTS, 5) ensure that the document outlines next steps for the recipient, 6) read the document in its entirety verbatim and provide the recipient with a copy, 7) have a witness (assistant principal whenever possible) present during the conference, 8) allow time for the recipient to respond during the conference, 9) obtain signatures at the conclusion of the conference (if the recipient refuses to sign; that's fine, just have your witness sign and indicate that the recipient refused to sign, and 10) try to keep the conference as short as possible, but allot the necessary time to address the issue at hand.

Puzzle Pieces (How Do I Fit In?)

One of the first things you will learn as a principal is the fact that you cannot do everything by yourself. That's why this role is referred to as the principalship, because you are going to need the assistance of many key individuals. Therefore, your role as principal will require you to invest the necessary time in communicating your vision for the campus and explaining to people how they fit into the "puzzle." Everyone at the school has a role to play in preparing students to be lifelong learners and contributors to society. Thus, it is important for each staff member to know what their role is and how it contributes to the overall success of the campus.

If Possible....NO VACANCIES ON THE FIRST DAY OF SCHOOL

Here is the disclaimer...even though I am advocating for no vacancies on the first day of school, I am not encouraging in any way for any principal to ever rush the hiring process. The hiring process is one of the most important responsibilities of a principal. If this is not done correctly on the frontend, the stress that comes along on the backend is frustrating and time consuming. If you are fortunate to be in a position to hire staff during the summer, consider that time sacred as you attempt to hire the best that you possibly can for your vacant position.

Closing Thought

One of the most important responsibilities of a principal is recommending candidates for hire. The impact that hiring has on a campus cannot be underestimated. Therefore, the decision to recommend someone for hire should not be taken lightly. Once you receive the keys to your new campus, spend the necessary time learning all of the staff members' strengths and weaknesses. While learning their strengths and weaknesses, consider ways to utilize the strengths of your staff for the overall betterment of the campus. For those who need additional support, as the campus leader it is your responsibility to provide them with professional development in their specific areas of opportunity. Continue to communicate to your staff members their important role in achieving campus goals.

Nonetheless, when crucial conversations are needed, remember to 1) be willing to have crucial conversations, 2) know your communication style, 3) be transparent, honest, and ethical, and 4) keep your eyes on the prize: what's best for student.

CHAPTER 5: SCHOOL RELATIONS & COMMUNICATIONS

One of the most important things I had to learn during my first-year as a principal was that communicating with stakeholders, articulating your campus' vision, and conducting campus tours and visits would take up a lot of your time; time that you don't have as a principal. Nonetheless, the time spent engaging in school public relations activities, as well as keeping open communication with all of your stakeholders is critical to your success as a principal. In other words, you don't have time, to not have time, to engage in school public relations. Unfortunately, in some communities, if this is not done well or correctly by the principal, it can be damaging to their career, regardless of how well the campus may perform academically. If there is any chapter that I would personally recommend a new principal to read in its entirety, it would be this one. Enjoy and take heed to this valuable information. Don't learn the hard way!!

Be Willing to Articulate Your Vision for the Campus

On more occasions than you would like, you are guaranteed to hear this question by visitors, prospective employees or students, community members, central office personnel, etc…. "so tell us about your campus." As principal, what is your vision for the campus? I highly recommend that all new principals have a short and succinct answer to this question. Being able to articulate the vision you have for your camps is critical to the overall success of the school. How can you expect your campus to be successful if you do not have a convincing vision? As a doctoral student, I was always told to have an "elevator speech" in which you are able to articulate the main components of your dissertation in a short period of time. Meaning, if you were speaking to someone on an elevator ride and you had to explain the main purpose of your dissertation before both of you arrived at your destination, what would you tell them? Principals should be able to do the same when it comes to articulating their campus' vision. Work hard on being able to highlight the key components of your school in less than one minute. Yes, this will require you to stay focused when speaking, but it will also ensure that you are articulating the most noteworthy aspects of your campus.

In addition to having a precise "elevator speech" in order to articulate your campus vision, I would recommend creating a brochure or pamphlet that you can provide to stakeholders during visits and/or meetings. Since your "elevator speech" is short and precise, a brochure or pamphlet will allow for stakeholders to read more about your campus, ask any follow-up questions that they may have, but ultimately, it would allow for you to continue "leading the conversation." As a first-year principal, if you are able to learn how to "lead conversations with stakeholders" you are ahead of many other principals both novice and experienced.

Ensure that Your Actions Align with Your Message

As the old adage goes, "your actions speak louder than your words" is a perfect description of the principalship. If someone were to ask me, "what is one thing you would tell a new principal that is usually never told to them before taking on the role" it would be just that. Everything that you *do* and *don't do* as a principal is evaluated, assessed, analyzed, critiqued, and dissected by people (who are in most cases your staff and/or stakeholders). Therefore, it is absolutely critical that you always keep that in mind when thinking about your actions and how they align or don't align with your message. You already know that as principal people are going to ask you to describe your philosophy when it comes to education, leadership, student learning, quality instruction, etc. You already know that people are going to ask you to describe your campus culture, demographics, successes, and challenges. That's why it is very important that your actions align with your message because if they don't, please believe that someone will recognize the misalignment.

Weekly Communication with Stakeholders

If all possible, please consider having some form of weekly communication with stakeholders. This communication can be sent electronically, hard-copy, posted somewhere in the building, etc. The main purpose for doing this, is to ensure that you are consistently keeping stakeholders informed about the wonderful things happening on your campus. As principal, I sent home a weekly newsletter entitled *Jaguar Journal* electronically, hard-copy, and posted it on the website. Every Tuesday, my families and community members knew that Dr. Waters was sending home the *Jaguar Journal* that highlighted what was happening on the campus for the week or upcoming weeks. The newsletter spotlighted a student, staff member, and college or university by identifying the location of the school, famous alum, and if anyone at the campus graduated from the institution.

Having weekly communication with parents decreased the number of questions that my front office staff had to answer regarding events, because stakeholders felt well informed and updated on a regular basis. In addition to the weekly newsletter, I kept my campus website and marquee updated with the most current information as well as the campus calendar posted when you first walked into the school building. These things may seem small at first glance, but having your stakeholders well informed is great publicity for your campus. Consider ways in which you will communicate with stakeholders on a weekly basis.

Take Advantage of Opportunities to Positively "Show Off" Your Campus

During the times in which we live, there is one thing for sure, you can watch any news broadcast and expect to hear something negative regarding the schools in your community, or throughout our country. Negative coverage about schools is one of the major attractions for local news stations. Therefore, as principal, you have to take advantage of any opportunity to have your campus spotlighted for the positive things going on. Take the time to build a relationship with the district's communications department as well as local media outlets. This will benefit you in the long run when you contact them about covering an event or special occasion on your campus. As a principal, I pray that you don't ever have to worry about the media portraying your school in a negative light, so take advantage of all of the positive publicity you can whenever you can, big or small.

Schedule Time Weekly for Face-to Face Conferences and Meetings

When you are given the keys to your building as principal, take a few moments to identify the day(s) and times you will conduct weekly face-to-face meetings or conferences with stakeholders. One thing that I did before school started each year was to identify the specific days and times in which I would have parent conferences or general meetings with individuals. It will not take you long to figure out that time is the most precious thing a principal does not have enough of. Therefore, if you are not careful, people will try to monopolize and take all of the little time that you really don't have. That's one of the main reasons why I decided to implement the process of having designated days and times for parent conferences. I selected times during the morning and afternoon in order to accommodate parents because of their work schedules. Despite having specific days and times, there are going to be instances when emergencies arise. I would always take those meetings quickly in order to handle the situation appropriately. As a principal, you never want to have your parents or stakeholders feeling as if they were not "heard." The last thing you want them to do is to call the district office and complain about poor customer service over something that you could have easily handled on your campus. That type of publicity or reputation is something you want to avoid as much as possible.

Monthly Parent and Campus-Based Decision Team Meetings

Depending on your geographical location, you may have a PTA, PTO, Site-Based Decision Making (SBDM) Team, etc. Nonetheless, you want to schedule time monthly to meet with these organizations and to keep them informed of what's happening at the campus. As previously mentioned, time is so precious to principals. Therefore, I scheduled my parent meetings and site-based decision making team meetings on the same day. The first meeting was the

SBDM followed by PTA. This allowed for me to not only share updates and get feedback from stakeholders, but I was able to maximize the opportunity of engaging with them while they were already on campus.

One of the best tricks that I learned when it came to getting parents out to PTA meetings was to 1) provide food, 2) have a raffle for parents to win prizes, and 3) schedule grade-level student performances. Parents always came out when food was being provided, when they had an opportunity to win something, and most importantly to see their child perform. My parent participation numbers skyrocketed when I implemented those three ideas. I highly recommend thinking about ways to get your stakeholders on campus monthly in order to continue keeping the lines of communication open.

Communicating with Campus Personnel

For the majority of this chapter I have written about the importance of communicating regularly with parents, community members, and other stakeholders. It is also extremely important to ensure that you communicate regularly and honestly with your staff. In addition to having a weekly communication system in place for your stakeholders, you may want to consider having a weekly memo that is sent to your staff on a specific day. This is an area that I wished I would have focused a little more of my attention. There are some principals who are really good at providing their staff with weekly memos. A major advantage to doing this is when you consider your staff meetings. If you are planning on meeting with your staff on a weekly, biweekly, or monthly basis, consider having a weekly memo that is sent to all of your staff electronically. In that memo, you can provide the staff with all of the major updates, remind them of deadlines, provide feedback on what you are noticing on the campus, etc. This would in turn allow for you to not spend most of your staff meetings providing announcements or updates, but you will actually be able to spend time conducting and engaging in professional development. My philosophy is, "whenever all of the staff is together, this is a perfect time to provide them with something that will result in them leaving the meeting more equipped to prepare students for success than when they arrived." I highly recommend and would encourage you to consider all of the different systems you would create to ensure that communication with your staff is consistent, honest, and transparent.

Closing Thought

The importance of school public relations is critical to the success of any principal. As principal, you have to maintain consistent, honest, and transparent communication with all stakeholders. Continue to work on your elevator speech as a principal in order to communicate your campus' vision in a succinct manner. Keep in mind that actions speak louder than words, so as a principal you want to remain mindful of your actions and how they align with your words/beliefs. Always consider ways to establish relationships with district, community people, and the local media. This will pay dividends during your tenure as a principal. Consider hosting parent meetings on a monthly basis in order to keep your stakeholders informed of what is happening on your campus. Having a weekly schedule in place to meet with your campus leadership team, departments, etc. is another way to keep everyone on the "same page."

CHAPTER 6: DESIGNING YOUR 90-DAY PLAN

We have considered the following aspects of the principalship so far: 1) culture and climate, 2) instructional leadership, 3) school personnel administration, and 4) school public relations/communications. These are the main areas that principals must consider when creating their 90-day plans. The purpose of this chapter is to provide recommendations for consideration when designing your 90-day plan.

You have the Keys…Now What? (July - August)

A recommended objective for the first 30 days of your 90-day plan is to: "establish relationships with community members and campus personnel." During my first week as a new principal, I sent out an email to all of the staff inviting them to come and meet me (if they were available) during a two-week period. It was on a voluntary basis because they were still on summer vacation. To my surprise, over 90% of the staff scheduled time to meet with me. These meetings were very beneficial. I was able to learn more about my staff as well as the culture and climate of the campus. As previously mentioned in chapter 2, I asked all of the staff the same four questions: 1) what worked well, 2) what didn't work, 3) what is one thing you would change immediately, and 4) what are your expectations of me as your principal? Having those meetings was advantageous for me as a new principal because, the information that I received in two weeks, would have taken six weeks if I wouldn't have taken the time to open up my schedule. Therefore, we were able to start off the school year strong as a new team, because of the short time I invested over the summer learning about the culture of the campus and trying to build relationships. Here are a few items that you may want to consider when identifying action steps for the first 90-days.

Meet with immediate supervisor to analyze data and create goals for school year	Meet with Campus Leadership Team
Invite all staff members to an one-on-one meetings on a voluntary basis	Send Principal Introduction and Welcome Letter to Staff, Parents, and Students (multiple languages if necessary)
Finalize personnel positions and vacancies	Ensure that all instructional material is ready for staff return
Meet with SBDM and PTA/Community Members	Finalize Campus Handbook and School Calendar

Visibility Leads To Credibility (August - September)

One of my favorite sayings is "Visibility leads to Credibility."
As a principal you have to be visible throughout your building and
community whenever possible. During the first 60 days, you want to
be visible each day your school building is open. Of course there are
going to be times when you have to attend meetings off campus,
attend workshops, etc. Nonetheless, when the school building is
open, you need to be mindful that you are not spending too much
time in your office. Schedule your day so that you can be seen
throughout your building, in the hallways, during arrival and
dismissal times, etc. This is the period when school is starting back
after the summer break. Therefore, you are going to have to get your
expectations and procedures communicated to your students and
staff quickly and efficiently. Utilize this time to explain non-
negotiables and model expectations. This process is going to be
critical as you move into the next 30 days. Here are some action
items that you may want to consider accomplishing within the first
60 days of your principalship.

Send "Back to School" Letters to all Families and Staff Members (multiple languages if necessary)	Host "Meet and Greet" Night with New Principal (1st week of school or before)
Host Grade Level Assemblies during 1st Week of School to explain campus-wide expectations	Continue being "visible" and set expectations from morning rituals to end of the school day procedures.
Conduct informal classroom observations and provide timely feedback and support	Host a "Back to School Night" for families to meet faculty and staff (1st Week of School)
Weekly staff meetings to establish and reinforce norms and expectations. Also to provide professional development, updates on action plan goals, and reiterate school and district core beliefs.	Ensure that your campus curriculum alignment is strong in preparation for the first set of campus-based assessments

The Honeymoon is Over…. Here Comes the Data (September –

October)

Okay, the honeymoon is over…. here comes the first round of

common assessment or campus-based assessment data! You have

completed your first 90-days as a principal and now you have to take

an in-depth look at where your campus is academically. The data is

in!! Don't stress if your data did not come out the way you would

have hoped, think of your action plan and how you are going to

address the weak areas, as well as advance in the areas where student are excelling. As principal, you have to keep in mind that all of your students should be taken into consideration when creating your action plan to address achievement data. Meaning, there should be a plan created that would allow for your students who are excelling academically to move further ahead. For your students who are on the cusp of passing, there should be a plan in place to move them over the hump. As for your students who are further behind and struggling, there should be a plan in place for them to demonstrate academic growth. Below are some ideas to include in your 90-day plan once the data has been received and analyzed.

Continue conducting informal and formal classroom observations and providing instructional feedback and support to teachers	Ensure that teachers are continuing to follow the curriculum alignment map in preparation for standardized assessments
Analyze common assessment data on a regular basis and create action plans based off the data (data-driven instruction)	Meet regularly with grade levels to discuss data (academic and behavior) and create plans to address concerns in a timely manner
Begin incorporating standard-based tutorials (afterschool and/or Saturday sessions)	Provide differentiated staff development training based off campus data and teacher need.
Conduct an interim culture and climate survey in order to identify areas of praise and opportunities for growth before the spring semester.	Host a "State of the School" Staff Meeting to provide updates on action plans

Tips to Remember When Designing Your 90-Day Plan

Whenever I am presenting or helping aspiring administrators create their 90-day plan, the first thing that I highly encourage them to do is to ensure that they "**<u>IMPLEMENT THEIR 90-DAY PLAN!!</u>**" I cannot stress this enough. Don't spend time creating a 90-day plan when you are preparing for an interview and after creating it, place it on a bookshelf to collect dust. NO! Take those same ideas that you thought of, and begin implementing them after you have been named the principal or assistant principal for your new campus. As a person who has been on the committee to select new principals for campuses, I can attest that if your interview process requires you to complete a 90-day plan that you will present to the search committee, you can rest assure that the information that you present will carry a lot of weight when it comes to making the final hiring recommendation. Not only that, those on the search committee will wonder if you are actually going to implement the strategies or ideas that you mentioned during your 90-day plan presentation.

In addition, during conference presentations or when I am working personally with an aspiring and/or new administrator to create their 90-day plan, I encourage them to "enjoy the process!" Here is a low-risk opportunity for you to create a plan of action for a campus that you are not responsible for, so take advantage of the experience of "thinking like a principal." This is a great time for you to begin thinking about some of the things you would do to kick-off your experience as a principal during your first 90-days. Below are a few tips that I would encourage aspiring and/or new principals to keep in mind when designing their 90-day plan.

· If given the task to create a 90-day plan as an interview requirement for a principal or assistant principal position, **analyze the data that the committee provides carefully and thoroughly.** There are specific areas (based off the data) that the committee is interested in hearing your thoughts about. For example, if the data shows that a specific population of students in your building are struggling in a content area, highlight that in your plan, and create action steps that will allow for you to address those deficiencies.

· **Think of the 90-day plan as Units**. The first unit being the first 30 days, the second the next 30 days, and the last the final 30 days. This will help you compartmentalize your thoughts and actions, therefore creating a more logical and sequential 90-day plan.

Continue to ask yourself, "what do I want my campus and myself to accomplish by the end of this 90-day period?"

· **<u>Ensure Feasibility and Practicality</u>.** Remember, I am a strong proponent for administrators creating a 90-day plan and actually implementing it. Therefore, when you create your 90-day plan, please consider action steps that are feasible and practical. These are things that you know you can actually do. Refrain from including action steps that are too elaborate or unrealistic. Show the committee or your staff that your 90-day plan is attainable and you are confident that your skillset will allow for you to complete the specified tasks.

· **<u>Focus on Learning and Responding Quickly</u>.** Your 90-day plan should have a strong focus on learning more about your staff, students, and stakeholders. There should be a strong indication in your 90-day plan that you are taking the time to learn more about those you are entrusted to serve. In addition, your 90-day plan should also focus on identifying key leverage areas within your school that impacts campus culture/climate, instructional delivery, and student achievement. After identifying those areas, it is imperative that you have a plan and respond quickly.

Closing Thought

The best piece of advice that I can give anyone who is preparing their first 90-day plan as a newly appointed principal is to "WORK YOUR PLAN!" I cannot emphasize this enough. Don't waste your time creating a plan if you are not going to implement it with fidelity. I also encourage those creating a 90-day plan to enjoy the process. Enjoy the process of brainstorming and strategizing your steps as a new administrator. The creation and implementation of a 90-day plan can be overwhelming. In order to ease the pressure of feeling overwhelmed, you may want to consider viewing your 90-day plan in units. By doing so, you are ensuring that your plan is feasible, practical, and focused on teaching and learning.

CHAPTER 7: JUDGEMENT DAY & PURPOSEFUL PLANNING

Depending on your start date as a new principal, your "judgement day" after your first 90-days is going to vary. For the most part, if you begin your journey during the summer, the completion of your first 90-days is going to be around the first or second week in October. As a rule of thumb for me, I always considered October 1st as my "Judgment Day." Judgment day in the sense that, you have completed your first 90-days and now you have to take time to celebrate "small wins" as well as reflect on your areas for growth. This chapter focuses on the need to be reflective, honest, and forward-thinking about your first 90-days in order to have a strong finish to the school year.

Reflect and Be Honest about the First 90-Days

If you can't be honest with anyone, this is the time to be honest with yourself. You have been in your position for 90-days and you have truly learned something in your new role. Take the necessary time to revisit your 90-day plan and reflect on your successes and areas of opportunity. Remember the importance of celebrating the "little wins" throughout your journey, but also have a plan in place for those areas that need more attention. It is without question that your first 90-days are going to be filled with wonderful accomplishments, but you are going to have some challenges ahead. Reflect on and learn from those experiences. Don't let difficult days dictate your next 90-days. Consider creating a personal and professional plan of action to address the inevitable challenges ahead, while using them as learning experiences.

Ask for Honest and Constructive Feedback from Campus Leadership Team

Okay, so you've had the opportunity to personally reflect on the first 90-days of your principalship. Now, you should consider taking the leap of faith by asking for honest and constructive feedback from your campus leadership team. This is an opportunity to get another perspective on your first 90-days, while also brainstorming with your leadership team on next steps. While asking for feedback from your campus leadership team, please encourage them to be honest and constructive with their feedback. Now is not the time for them to tell you what you want to hear; you need to hear the good along with the bad. Don't take everything personally. Consider ways in which you can continue moving the campus forward as the principal, while also soliciting the ideas and assistance from your leadership team. The response that you get from your campus leadership team may surprise you. Nonetheless, take a moment to reflect on their feedback, keep in mind those high leverage areas, remember that everything that needs to take place should focus on doing what's best for students. I highly encourage you to solicit not only feedback from your campus leadership team, but have them provide you with solutions or recommendations as well.

I remember going into the office of the Chief Academic Officer in my district and on her white board she had a quote which read, "don't come to the table with problems, come with opportunities to lead." This is what you want your campus leadership team to keep in mind when providing honest feedback regarding the first 90-days. As principal, you need a leadership team that consists of individuals who want the best for students, and who are willing to work diligently to increase student academic achievement by improving teaching and learning.

Personal and Professional Development Plans

Every year throughout my career, I have always created personal and professional development plans. The purpose of these plans are to keep me focused on continuing to develop my capacity in the area of school leadership. Education as an industry is always changing. Therefore, it is imperative for professional educators to seek out new trainings, and to remain abreast on the current literature in the field. Despite rapid societal changes, education as an industry does a poor job of keeping pace with global advancements. Knowing this, I personally invest the time and energy to keep my professional training aligned with global trends. I highly encourage all administrators to create personal and professional development plans each year. Having a detailed plan that outlines specific actions and areas of your leadership that you would like to improve, will have a tremendous impact on your students and staff.

Recently I heard a sports announcer explain NBA star Steph Curry's summer training ritual. He stated that Steph Curry would pick an area of his game that he wanted to focus on during the off-season and perfect it before the new season begins. As a result, Steph Curry has improved his game so much that he has become a "household name," MVP of the league, and two-time NBA champion. Just imagine how great of a principal you could become if you would identify an area of your leadership that you would like to improve and seek out professional development trainings specifically in that area. If you commit to doing this each year, the positive impact you can have as a campus leader could be astronomical.

Personnel Changes (Act Quickly and Professionally)

The time has come. During your 90-day tenure, you have assessed yourself as an administrator and the personnel on your campus. If you are truly fortunate, 100% of your staff is doing a fantastic job and you want to keep everyone who comes to work each day. On the contrary, if you are like the majority of principals, you have some people on your staff that are not a "good fit" for your campus. As result, you should consider obtaining and organizing the necessary paperwork to make personnel changes. One bit of advice that I can give any novice administrator would be, when staff members demonstrate that they are not a "good fit" for the campus, believe them, then act quickly and professionally. I cannot overstate this. Don't waste your time as an administrator with staff members who are unwilling to increase their capacity for the sake of student learning. I encourage any principal to provide support to struggling personnel, but after the support has been rendered and if the staff member is unable to demonstrate any improvements, then it is time to seek guidance from your district's human resources department to inquire about the process of recommending a staff member for non-renewal or termination. Nonetheless, it is imperative for the campus principal to remain professional and act quickly when it comes to making such a recommendation.

Closing Thought

At the conclusion of your first 90-days, I encourage you to spend some time reflecting and being honest. Think about the job you have done and ask for honest constructive feedback from stakeholders. Revisit your personal and professional PD plans. This will allow for you to identify areas that you want to continue working on for the remainder of the school year. As always, keep in mind that if any personnel changes need to be made, please ensure that you work quickly and professionally to submit those recommendations with the human resources department. Keep in mind that the academic well-being of your students depend on it.

CHAPTER 8: CONCLUSION & RECOMMENDATIONS

Before the last word is typed, I think it is important for me to revisit the purpose of the text. At the conclusion of my first-year as a principal, I reflected on the many things that I learned via "trial and error." As I mentioned previously, I did not receive a lot of support from the district-level when it came to making the transition into the princiaplship. That is one of the main reasons why I decided to focus my dissertation research on first-year principals' transition into their new role. While completing my dissertation, I realized the importance of taking that newfound research information and then creating some practical tips for new and/or aspiring administrators. That belief inspired me to write this book. The sole purpose of this book is to provide new and/or aspiring principals with tips and recommendations that I wished I would have known prior to, or during, my first principal assignment. My goal was to write the text in a conversational manner so that the information would be easily understood and enjoyable to read. I wanted the reader to feel as if we were having a conversation about the topics addressed and not reading a textbook or typical leadership book.

In addition to reflecting on my first-year as a principal, I spent time thinking about my professional career path towards the principalship. I thought about my experiences as a teacher and when I began thinking about moving into a campus leadership role. Therefore, this chapter will provide some recommendations for teachers who are ready to take that "leap" into administration. Also included in this chapter are recommendations for assistant principals who are ready to take that "leap" into becoming the head-principal, and superintendents or principal supervisors responsible for working with new administrators.

Recommendations for Teachers

As a classroom teacher, you will experience some excitement and anxiety when you begin considering going into administration. I remember when I felt the time was right for me to take principal certification courses as a teacher. I was young and believed that anyone could be a principal. Boy was I wrong! The first piece of advice that I would give teachers who are considering becoming an assistant principal or principal is to get as much exposure as possible with leadership opportunities on your campus. This is critical. There are so many aspects of campus leadership that you do not see as a teacher. Therefore, taking on leadership roles within the campus will allow for you to experience "the other side" of school operations. Personally speaking, I became a better teacher and more appreciative of my administrators once I began taking on campus leadership roles. I was able to see first-hand the many challenges faced by campus leaders on a daily basis.

In addition, I would recommend any teacher who wants to become an administrator to seek out a mentor and ask to "shadow" them periodically. Spending time observing an administrator in action, and having an opportunity to ask questions is helpful when making the transition into campus leadership. The more time you spend observing and asking questions related to your desired new role, the better equipped you will feel as you take your required courses and apply for vacant campus administrator positions. Lastly, you know I couldn't finish this section without mentioning the importance of creating a tentative 90-day plan as you continue learning and growing as a school leader.

Recommendations for Assistant Principals

You are almost there, one step away from becoming a campus principal. If you haven't done so already, it is very important for you to begin thinking about your 90-day plan as you mentally prepare for the transition into the principalship. If you are an assistant principal, most likely you have completed the necessary coursework and/or certification requirements to become a campus principal. Therefore, your main focus should be on continuing to gain valuable experiences by serving as summer school principal, learning more about state assessment coordination, taking advantage of opportunities to learn more about campus budgeting, etc. You are now seeking out opportunities to increase your leadership capacity as you move forward in your quest of becoming a principal.

Another recommendation for assistant principals aspiring to become principals is to continue networking with district-level personnel. Take advantage of opportunities to interact with area superintendents and/or the district's superintendent. Conduct yourself in a manner in which you are "interviewing every day." Meaning, you never know who is watching you and considering you for administrator vacancies. Having a positive professional reputation will go a long way during your quest to advance your career.

Recommendations for Superintendents

As a superintendent, you have the responsibility of working with campus principals with varying backgrounds. While working on my superintendent certification, I always kept in mind that one of the most important responsibilities associated with the superintendency, is the ability to continuously increase the leadership capacity of campus principals. During my first-year as a principal, I was intrigued by the amount of training and professional development that the superintendent personally provided to principals. I can honestly say that he believed wholeheartedly that in order to increase student academic achievement, school principals must be equipped with specific leadership competencies. In order to acquire these competencies and to become the best instructional leader possible, principals should be provided with ongoing professional development and support.

Furthermore, I encourage superintendents to work closely with all of their campus leaders, especially first-year principals. Despite how successful a first-year principal was as an assistant principal; superintendents cannot take for granted that their previous success will automatically transfer into the principalship without support.

Superintendents should remain mindful of the equitable needs of their first-year principals and provide support accordingly. Please remember, first-year principals will need assistance from district-level personnel and they should never be left alone to "sink or swim."

Closing Thought

Teachers, as you begin to make your transition into campus administration, continue to seek out opportunities that will enhance your leadership skills. This will make you more marketable during your job search for administrative positions. Assistant principals, start working on your 90-day plan immediately, while continuing to seek out additional opportunities to broaden your leadership skillset. Superintendents, your role is critical. The support that you provide to your principals should be ongoing and equitable based off need. Please don't leave your principals (new or seasoned) in the trenches to either "sink or swim."

References

Business Dictionary. http://www.businessdictionary.com

Dufour, R. & Marzano, R. (2011). *Leaders of learning: How district, school, and classroom leaders improve student achievement.* Solution Tree Press.

Glossary of Education Reform. http://edglossary.org

National School Climate Council. http://www.schoolclimate.org/climate

Waters, D. (2017). Principals and crucial conversations. *Texas Elementary Principals and Supervisors Association, v (30), no.2, 9-12.*

58919234R00063

Made in the USA
San Bernardino, CA
30 November 2017